NEWCASTLE/BLOODAXE POETRY SERIES: 7

JANE HIRSHFIELD:
HIDDENNESS, UNCERTAINTY, SURPRISE

NEWCASTLE/BLOODAXE POETRY SERIES

1: Linda Anderson & Jo Shapcott (eds.)
Elizabeth Bishop: Poet of the Periphery

2: David Constantine: *A Living Language*
NEWCASTLE / BLOODAXE POETRY LECTURES

3: Julia Darling & Cynthia Fuller (eds.)
The Poetry Cure

5: Carol Rumens: *Self into Song*
NEWCASTLE / BLOODAXE POETRY LECTURES

6: Desmond Graham: *Making Poems and Their Meanings*
NEWCASTLE / BLOODAXE POETRY LECTURES

7: Jane Hirshfield: *Hiddenness, Uncertainty, Surprise*
NEWCASTLE / BLOODAXE POETRY LECTURES

8: Ruth Padel: *Silent Letters of the Alphabet*
NEWCASTLE / BLOODAXE POETRY LECTURES

9: George Szirtes: *Fortinbras at the Fishhouses*
NEWCASTLE / BLOODAXE POETRY LECTURES

10: Fiona Sampson: *Music Lessons*
NEWCASTLE / BLOODAXE POETRY LECTURES

11: Jackie Kay, James Procter & Gemma Robinson (eds.)
Out of Bounds: British Black & Asian Poets

12: Sean O'Brien: *Journeys to the Interior*
NEWCASTLE / BLOODAXE POETRY LECTURES

13: Paul Batchelor (ed.)
Reading Barry MacSweeney

14: John Halliday (ed.)
Don't Bring Me No Rocking Chair: poems on ageing

15: Gwyneth Lewis: *Quantum Poetics*
NEWCASTLE / BLOODAXE POETRY LECTURES

16: Anne Stevenson: *About Poems and how poems are not about*
NEWCASTLE / BLOODAXE POETRY LECTURES

17: Carolyn Forché & Jackie Kay (eds.)
The Mighty Stream: poems in celebration of Martin Luther King

NEWCASTLE/BLOODAXE POETRY SERIES: 7

JANE HIRSHFIELD

Hiddenness, Uncertainty, Surprise:

Three Generative Energies of Poetry

NEWCASTLE / BLOODAXE POETRY LECTURES

BLOODAXE BOOKS

ISBN: 978 1 85224 797 3

First published 2008 by
Newcastle Centre for the Literary Arts,
Newcastle University,
Newcastle upon Tyne NE1 7RU,
in association with
Bloodaxe Books Ltd,
Eastburn,
South Park,
Hexham,
Northumberland NE46 1BS.

www.bloodaxebooks.com
For further information about Bloodaxe titles
please visit our website and join our mailing list
or write to the above address for a catalogue.

Supported using public funding by
**ARTS COUNCIL
ENGLAND**

Cover design: Neil Astley & Pamela Robertson-Pearce.

Digital reprint of the 2008 Bloodaxe Books edition

Contents

Acknowledgements

Jane Hirshfield wishes to thank Newcastle University for the invitation to deliver these three essays as the Newcastle / Bloodaxe Lectures in March 2007. She also wishes to thank the venues for whom earlier versions of these thoughts were first developed: The Rochester Arts and Lectures Series ('Poetry and Hiddenness: Thoreau's Hound', May 2001) and the Napa Valley Writers Conference ('Poetry and Uncertainty', July 2003, and 'Poetry and the Constellation of Surprise', July 2005). Earlier versions of these essays appeared in *The American Poetry Review* and *The Associated Writing Programs Chronicle*.

Poetry and Hiddenness: Thoreau's Hound

'I long ago lost a hound, a bay horse, and a turtle dove, and am still on their trail. Many are the travelers I have spoken to concerning them, describing their tracks and what calls they answered to. I have met one or two who had heard the hound, and the tramp of the horse, and even seen the dove disappear behind a cloud, and they seemed as anxious to recover them as if they had lost them themselves.' These much quoted words are Henry David Thoreau's, from *Walden*. And here is a sentence, different yet not unrelated, from his friend and neighbor Emerson's essay, 'Experience' – 'Sleep lingers all our lifetime about our eyes, as night hovers all day in the boughs of the fir tree.'

Homo sapiens sapiens: the name defines a species that wants to *know*. Yet a counter-thirst exists in us as well, for something the opposite of knowledge, of too easy exposure. Who would think Emerson's fir tree more beautiful if the darkness were stripped from its depths, or prefer Thoreau's elusive turtle dove caged and in hand? 'Heard melodies are sweet,' wrote Keats, 'but those unheard are sweeter.' A fidelity to the ungraspable lies at the very root of both biological existence and what we experience as beauty; the steepest pitches of the heart and mind make their own shade. Within that cool and dimness, emotions and thoughts small as new mosses and lichens begin the slow, green colonisations of incipient life.

Concealment does not presume conscious intention. Perspective, though, is essential: hiddenness requires the presence of both a seer and something that might be seen. The English word for hiding is sewn into the hides of animals bodies; both derive from Old German and Sanskrit terms for protection. The German *huota* lingers on in the intimate dwelling place that is a 'hut'. Hiddenness, then, is a sheltering enclosure – though one we stand some times outside of, at others within. One of its homes is the Ryoan-ji rock garden in Kyoto: wherever in it a person stands, one of the fifteen rocks cannot be seen. The garden reminds that something unknowable is always present in a life, just beyond what can be perceived or comprehended – yet that something is as much part of the real as any other stone amid the raked gravel. It is our subjectivity of stance, not the world, that creates the unknown.

In Western literature, explorations of hiddenness go back to the beginning. The largest hiddenness and initial mystery is that which surrounds birth and death, and the central axis of our earliest extant epic, the Sumerian *Gilgamesh*, is the unhiding of death to human perception. To know we must cross death's ungainsayable threshhold is the price of entrance to full consciousness – self-awareness is needed to recognise the vanishing of selves. The realisation of our lives as at once separate, interconnected, and transient propels Gilgamesh's outcry upon his friend Enkidu's death, 'This will happen also to me!' In that moment lies one division between animal-consciousness and the fully human – while animals may feel, may dream, may solve, may mourn, it does not seem they grapple with the foreknowledge of death. Only we live face to face with that walled-up gate, whose through-passing makes us who we are.

Hiddenness saturates the works of the Greeks. The tragedies turn on the wheel-rim of an incomplete knowledge, compassion, or vision, and concealments both shadow and charge the Homeric epics. The *Odyssey*, in particular, can be read as a study of hiddenness in a human life: the way it can, rightly welcomed, develop and temper our nature. An odd symmetry of disappearance marks the opening of each of the epics. After the *Iliad*'s initiating quarrel, the hero Achilles retires to his tent, not to reemerge for another eight books. For the first four books of the *Odyssey*, Odysseus is similarly unseen: he has been 'banished into black obscurity' in the goddess Calypso's grottoes. During his subsequent wanderings, Odysseus is dipped repeatedly into the condition of the unseen. He is concealed in dense thorn bushes and mists; he escapes the cave of the Cyclops Polyphemus by suspending himself beneath the belly of a thick-wooled ram;

when he finally reenters Ithaca it is disguised in the rags of an aged beggar. This is not the first time. When the man of craft, as he is called, scouts the city of Troy before executing his plan for the Trojan Horse – another stratagem of invisibility, it need hardly be noted – he also dresses as a beggar, to the point of covering himself in self-inflicted bruises. Who would look for a hero in such battered form?

The Homeric poems are filled with event and drama, sea-storms and battles. Yet the stories turn on strategic or sullen withdrawals, on the threshold-moments when things are not what they seem. A king and a warrior each behave like a spoiled child. A wooden horse is abandoned on a beach by a seemingly departed army. A far-travelling hero learns to trust no one, to lie about his name and history, to receive the abuse of a goat-herd and keep his tongue silent. Even the goddess Athena, entering into human events at various times to ensure an outcome, disguises herself in the form of a shepherd or serving girl or long-trusted friend. When the gods appear in the world of ordinary beings, they borrow the shapes of the earth.

Achilles in the cloak of his tent, Odysseus wrapped in his guise of beggar are each persons removed from their identities and signature powers. Achilles, though, emerges from his angry retreat essentially the same man, while Odysseus learns from the fabric of hiddenness a new power: he learns that fabrication in itself is power. Over the course of his long journey, he grows increasingly skillful at knowing what stories to speak aloud, what facts to keep shielded by silence. The man of craft – learning to suppress his old reliance on courage and boldness alone, learning to govern his tongue and its words – is the one who eludes the tragic hero's fate, who returns again to his place amid family and kingdom.

The lesson runs deep in both literature and the psyche: survival depends on an intimate and skillful comfort with similitude and disguise. The response of a biologist friend I asked to muse on the subject of hiddenness helps illumine why this is so:

> It's worth pointing out that for most of life on the planet, being hidden is the default condition. Visibility typically costs you your life, or at least a good meal. Sex or an advertisement of a poisonous

disposition are the only reasons anything with a pulse and a wink of sense would want to be conspicuous. This is why we are generally disappointed when we don our Vibram soles and trek through ticks and prickly shrubs to view wildlife. Wildlife are usually annoyed at being seen, if they are seen at all. As hiddenness is the default, visibility is a luxury. Rarely are earth-colored tones the symbols of opulence and royal blood. We are most comfortable being hidden but we yearn to be seen.[1]

The inventions of biological hiddenness are countless, witty, wily, and poignant. Insects mimic twigs and flower parts, the sexual partners or foods of their prey, whatever is poisonous to those for whom they themselves are prey. Flowers seeking fertilisation take the form and scents of the sexual partners of insects. A cohort of caterpillars bands together to travel in a long column, mirroring the body of a large and dangerous snake. There are spiders that look like bird droppings, pipe fish that sleep vertically to blend with surrounding reeds. Octopus and cuttlefish change the colors and texture of their skins to match the surfaces over which they travel; a jellyfish hides in its own transparence. Motion and motionlessness, too, can be shelter: minute water organisms, whose predators know them by the disturbance they make in the water, become cryptic by holding still. The same squid that first hides in the camouflage of protective coloration will, further threatened, jet swiftly away, but leaves behind a shadow-body of ink: highly visible, if substanceless decoy.

In the arts, the breadth of inventive disguise is much the same. To plunge one thing into the shape or nature of another is a fundamental gesture of creative insight, part of how we make for ourselves a world more expansive, deft, fertile, and startling in richness. The borrowing of attributes found in lyric image, metaphor, and parable is also one of the principles of sympathetic magic, a way to attempt to nudge the hand of chance or fate. A small example can be found in the Hoxne Hoard, a collection of fifth-century Roman treasure dug up in a Suffolk field in 1992 by a man who set out looking for a friend's lost hammer. Among the objects is the gold handle of a pouring vessel in the shape of a leaping tigress, heavy teats swelling down from the arc of her body. The sight pleases in its unexpected grace. It is also a promise of abundance – the principle of correspondence proposes that the vessel with such a handle, like the body of an actual nursing tigress, will not be emptied without that emptying causing it to refill.

To see the tigress hiding within a handle, the handle waiting within the tigress, is to throw off the boundaries of the literal and recognise that even the simplest fragment of existence can carry multiple uses, possibilities, connections. The union, like all metaphor, brings revelation and addition, as it also covers, complicates, veils. Art amplifies intelligence: to experience the tiger's gold-sculpted resonance is to join in the leap the mind must take towards a more sophisticated comprehension of the world. And that leap into new comprehension is also the difference between the more overt simile and the way a rightly realised metaphor affects us – to say that a handle is 'like a tiger' would merely perplex, but to make of a handle a bounding tigress is to enter the dream world where all things mysteriously conjoin.

'Our seeing is a mirror or a sieve,' wrote Zbigniew Herbert, in a poem meditating upon the sense of touch. The statement is eight words long, yet to unfold its two alternative metaphors fully would require passage through neuroscience, epistemology, personal psychology, and the grief of the self's inadequacy before words. Aristotle, in his *Rhetoric*, alludes to the kinship between metaphor and riddle, naming each a source for the other.[2] Not only does the solving of riddle depend on the ability to think metaphorically, all metaphor preserves some of the flavor of a puzzle. A metaphor simultaneously creates and solves its own riddle, and in that tiny explosion of mind is both expansion and release. Perhaps this is why, among the earliest poems in many traditions, riddles abound, and also why so much spiritual teaching partakes of the riddling: it is how the mind instructs itself in a more complex seeing. Probably the most famous of Western riddles is the one posed by the Sphinx and answered by Oedipus: 'What is it that walks on four legs at morning, two at midday, three at evening?' The answer of course is 'man', who crawls as an infant, walks upright in adulthood, and uses a cane in old age. The latent meaning that follows quietly behind, like a large dog at leashless heel, is this: Man is the creature who solves or fails to solve riddles. If he fails, he will die; if he succeeds, it will not release him from suffering, but he will be fully human.

Here is another small example, translated by Richard Wilbur from the seventh-century Anglo-Saxon of Aldhelm, abbot of Malmesbury and author of a collection of 101 rhyming riddles:

> Once I was white, full of scaly fish,
> But now am something else, by Fortune's wish.
> Through fiery torment I was made to grow
> as white as ashes, or as glinting snow.[3]

Even in this small quatrain about water and ice (a favored subject of medieval riddles), torment, transformation, and the hint of a full worldview – in the reference to 'Fortune' – are present. It is the nature of riddles, and metaphors, to exceed their apparent terrain, to teach us also to exceed the apparent. In the koans of Zen, the curriculum is explicit: 'Show me your face,' one famous example requests, 'before your parents were born.'

Mystery, secrecy, camouflage, silence, stillness, shadow, distance, opacity, withdrawal, namelessness, erasure, encryption, enigma, darkness, absence – these are the kaleidoscope names of the hidden, each carrying its particular description of something whose essence it is to elude describing. It is not surprising the trope of hiddenness appears in the realm of spiritual traditions as well. In certain Sufi and Kabbalistic traditions, the divine Face is said to have hidden itself in the fragmented world. Certain Tibetan Buddhist sutras, called *termas*, are texts believed once hidden for future revelation, given into the care of the *naga* dragon deities living deep in the earth, oceans, or lakes, or left deliberately in a cave for later discovery. It is easy to dismiss such a fantastic story. Then we remember the Dead Sea Scrolls, dating from the first centuries of the Christian era and found in a cave by two Bedouin shepherds in 1947 while searching for a lost goat. The similarly ancient Nag Hammadi gnostic gospels were buried in a meter-tall jar in another cave, and discovered in 1945 by Egyptian brothers hunting nitrate to fertilise their garden. It is possible to begin to see a theme: people go looking for one thing, and find another. A lost hammer leads to a Roman treasure, a lost goat to a cache of spiritual texts. Perhaps, for something to be found, the only thing that matters is that there be searching – certainly that is the way in the writing of poems.

Riddle-mind, whether spiritual, psychological, or secular, awakens a long-strided intelligence, breaking thought loose from the habitual and the stolid. This may explain why the following poem by Jack Gilbert brings so much pleasure – it is a handle revealing its tigress. To read it is to feel oneself restored to some partially forgotten complexity and fullness of being – though the poem shows also how often, as with Odysseus, such restoration must be arrived at by a passage through longing, failure, and loss.

The Forgotten Dialect of the Heart

How astonishing it is that language can almost mean,
and frightening that it does not quite. *Love*, we say,
God, we say, *Rome* and *Michiko*, we write, and the words
get it wrong. We say *bread* and it means according
to which nation. French has no word for home,
and we have no word for strict pleasure. A people
in northern India is dying out because their ancient
tongue has no words for endearment. I dream of lost
vocabularies that might express some of what
we no longer can. Maybe the Etruscan texts would
finally explain why the couples on their tombs
are smiling. And maybe not. When the thousands
of mysterious Sumerian tablets were translated,
they seemed to be business records. But what if they
are poems or psalms? My joy is the same as twelve
Ethiopian goats standing silent in the morning light.
O Lord, thou art slabs of salt and ingots of copper,
as grand as ripe barley lithe under the wind's labor.
Her breasts are six white oxen loaded with bolts
of long-fibered Egyptian cotton. My love is a hundred
pitchers of honey. Shiploads of thuya are what
my body wants to say to your body. Giraffes are this
desire in the dark. Perhaps the spiral Minoan script
is not a language but a map. What we feel most has
no name but amber, archers, cinnamon, horses and birds.[4]

*

15

Something in us awakens and breathes more deeply when it feels the world to be thus supple in its transformations and meanings. This is the leavening in the words of the French poet Paul Éluard: 'There is another world, but it is in this one.' It is also the leavening in any piece of literature worth reading: only words that enlarge the realm of the possible merit the borrowing of attention from the living world, because they return us to the knowledge of its original amplitude.

Another of hiding's faces is that of hiding in plain sight. This is what the walking-stick insect is doing, what certain forms of irony do as well. It is impossible to think long about hiddenness without coming into the gravitational pull of Edgar Allan Poe, and impossible to contemplate open hiding without arriving at 'The Purloined Letter'. Twice in that story, an incriminating letter is concealed by being left baldly in view; twice, the device succeeds for a time, then ultimately fails. Part of Poe's purpose, in this story and elsewhere, is to instruct the reader in how an extraordinary discernment may see what ordinary discernment does not: not by force of conquest, but by making of hiddenness an ally. The lesson appears in miniature at the story's start, when the narrator and his friend Dupin are smoking companionably in Dupin's library in the gathering dusk. They have been silent together for an hour or more when the Prefect of the Parisian police, identified only by the initial G—, arrives. 'We had been sitting in the dark,' the narrator reports, 'and Dupin now arose for the purpose of lighting a lamp, but sat down again, without doing so, upon G—'s saying that he had called to consult [...] upon official business [...] "If it is any point requiring reflection," observed Dupin, as he forbore to enkindle the wick, "we shall examine it to better purpose in the dark."'

Even at the most seemingly superficial level, Poe's stories are cat-and-mouse toyings with hiddenness, with information withheld and given. Throughout his works, for no apparent reason, amid a flood of offered details some small one will be arbitrarily denied. By implying, for instance, that the Prefect is a person in need of only discreet allusion by his initial, Poe contrives to make G—, and so the whole story, appear not fictive, but actual. Why, the reader subliminally muses, would a fictional person require protection from being named? The small, deliberate obscurity creates a semblance of the three-dimensional real, with its directional light and cast shadows: in a world where something is hidden, what is revealed must exist. (The reader's relationship to the story shifts as well; he or she becomes an insider, one trusted to recognise the person behind the hint. 'Ah yes,' the reader thinks, 'Prefect G——, I have met him before.' As she has, in 'The Murders in the Rue Morgue'.)

Poe's stratagem points toward a larger dynamic: hiddenness itself gives weight. In the archetypal reaches of the psyche, whatever is treasure partakes of the secret. Concealed in attic or vault, the very essence of physical treasure is that it is sequestered, neither easily come by nor easily kept – consider the pyramids' riches, *Beowulf*'s dragon's buried hoard. Immaterial treasure borrows the pattern. Inspiration, for instance, is often placed into the structure of a preserving, unseen gestation. Robert Frost described this with his customary pith: 'One has to be secret in order to secrete.'[5]

As deliberate concealment conveys the sense of the real, mystery increases the conviction that there is meaning. The elusive – in life, in literature – raises knowledge-lust in us as a small, quick movement raises the hunting response in a cat. And the elusive exists at multiple levels. To turn again to Poe, the story 'The Gold Bug' investigates less the finding of actual treasure – though that search gives the story its initial surface drive – than the transformations of being by which it occurs. What engages the narrator's passion is not buried gemstones, but the process of arriving at clarity, at something revealed. Accident (the trickster-energy's contribution) plays its part – a piece of paper on which directions to a treasure were once placed in invisible ink is exposed by chance to heat. (Cold preserves, heat transforms, in the psyche as in the physical world.) Still, by halfway through the story, the treasure has been dug up and savored; as with 'The Purloined Letter', in which the letter is returned to its rightful owner long before the tale's conclusion, the overt outcome to the overt mystery is a trifle, tossed to the reader in passing. The real pleasure – as always in the murder mysteries, detective stories, comedies and tragedies of error of which we never seem to tire – is found in grappling with an existence that has not been made simple. These riddle-raising and riddle-unraveling stories appeal because they stand against and correct the impulse in us toward an overly rational abstraction. The savor of mystery teaches that details matter.

Yet Poe did not want only the real: he sought something both less and more than what can be arrived at by ordinary perception. 'The Descent into the Maelstrom', 'A Cask of Amontillado', 'The Pit and the Pendulum' scar the psyche more deeply than the more straightforward tales of terror because they are neither reducible to allegory nor plausibly true. Poe is a writer entranced not with Emerson's fir trees, but only with the shadows in their boughs. 'The mere imitation, however accurate, of what *is* in Nature,' he wrote, 'entitles no man to the sacred name of "Artist". ...We can, at any time, double the true beauty of an actual landscape by half closing our eyes as we look at it. The naked Senses sometimes see too little – but then *always* they see too much.' [6]

*

Many poems hold certain of their thoughts in invisible ink. Such words, unlike Poe's map, need never be fully exposed to be fully perceived. What is left unexpressed can affect the reader perhaps even more strongly than what has been explicitly stated, precisely because it is has not been already taken into conscious account. Lyric poetry rests on the pivot point of said and unsaid, of clarity and complexity presented in mysteriously counterbalancing proportion. Within poems of intricate surface, more often than not, some large and simple gesture can be found; within poems apparently simple, more often than not, are behind-stage resonances, overtones, hidden knowledges, doublings back. One Japanese proverb states 'Even the reverse has a reverse.' W.H. Auden called great art, 'clear thinking about complex feelings'. A poem of Auden's can serve well to examine how this complexity works, and how something entirely unexpressed can be nonetheless felt in a poem – 'Musée des Beaux Arts'.

Musée des Beaux Arts

About suffering they were never wrong,
The Old Masters: how well they understood
Its human position: how it takes place
While someone else is eating or opening a window or just walking
      dully along;
How, when the aged are reverently, passionately waiting
For the miraculous birth, there always must be
Children who did not specially want it to happen, skating
On a pond at the edge of the wood:
They never forgot
That even the dreadful martyrdom must run its course
Anyhow in a corner, some untidy spot
Where the dogs go on with their doggy life and the torturer's horse
Scratches its innocent behind on a tree.

In Brueghel's *Icarus*, for instance: how everything turns away
Quite leisurely from the disaster; the ploughman may
Have heard the splash, the forsaken cry,
But for him it was not an important failure; the sun shone
As it had to on the white legs disappearing into the green
Water; and the expensive, delicate ship that must have seen
Something amazing, a boy falling out of the sky,
Had somewhere to get to and sailed calmly on.[7]

The poem seems at first straightforward enough. It begins with
a statement about the Old Masters, then illustrates that statement
with examples. But the poem does not sit on this surface level of
point and illustration, it plunges towards depth as quickly as that
falling boy into the sea. At the risk of ignoring Robert Frost's
useful warning that explication consists of 'saying a poem over
again, only worse', let us try to expose a little of this poem's
subterranean power.

First, there is its sound-making. Rhymes and half-rhymes
thread their way through Auden's words like an irregular flash
of gold thread – the full rhymes of 'wrong' and 'along', 'waiting'
and 'skating', but also the subtler and at times visually buried
intercallings of 'tree' and 'leisurely', 'failure' and 'water', 'shone'
and 'on'. There is also the rhythm: long-strided, complex sen-
tences extend by semi-colon, colon, comma. On a drumbeat of
musically impeccable reasoning, the poem works its way toward

new understanding. Even a non-English speaker, listening to this poem, could hear the process of thought's consideration and fulfillment.

But what is that conclusion? Paraphrased, it's pancake thin. One could put it like this: 'Mundane life goes on, it swallows up even the most extraordinary individual disaster.' Not an un-interesting statement, but one with nothing of the resonance of Auden's poem, nor its sense of a revelation wrung from the world by deep contemplation, nor its undertow grief. At this level, one might call the poem a simplicity dressed in complex clothes – though even that much makes a difference. The frame of placing its central concept within the mind not of the writer, but of the old master painters, matters; the particularity of those paintings, with their precisely rendered images of children skating on frozen ponds, their dogs and horses, ploughing peasant farmers and high-masted sailing ships, matters. The abstract idea has been thoroughly embedded in actual life, and this makes the idea more than it was. We feel the rub of the itchy long-dead horse against the tree, and with it the rub of our own small, finite, and mortal human existence against the world of others, animate and inanimate, transient and lasting. The poem scours the reader with the knowledge the paintings themselves also hold: that each moment occurs once only, in all the vastness of time. And so reading it, an unexpected feeling, half tenderness, half terror, floods the heart: Aristotle's classic, cleansing catharsis.

There is something else though, I think: an extra pressure of meaning that infuses the poem because it infused its writer. Even if the reader does not consciously know the subtext is there, it affects her or him nonetheless. 'Musée des Beaux Arts' was written in December, 1938. Auden, an Englishman with no small sense of history, had lived in Berlin. Months before, the annex-ation of Austria had occurred; the ceding of the Czech Sudeten-lands to Germany had just been negotiated in Munich. One can guess that Auden knew something of what was already in place of terror, and had some sense of the increase of terror about to come: how it too would be swallowed by the oblivious world, as all things are. That, I believe, is the true source of the poem's bitterness, the serrative knife edge one feels when reading it through. The poem is as chillingly politically prescient as its more prominent sibling, Auden's 'September 1, 1939'. The weight of that impotent foreknowledge leans heavy as an invisible draft horse into this seemingly calm examination of centuries-old art.

*

As the making and solving of riddle creates intelligence, a distinctive self is created by mavigating a path between the desire for hiddenness and the wish both to see and be seen. In the Hebrew bible, birthgiving and the covering fig leaf – the creative capacity and the impulse toward hiding – arrive together. Descartes, devoted to discovery, was himself deeply secretive, and claimed for his life motto *Bene vixit, bene qui latuit*, 'He who lives well lives well hidden.' Yet the British psychologist D.W. Winnicott described the dilemma of childhood by saying, 'It is a joy to be hidden, but a disaster not to be found.' (One could say the same of the writer's minute meaning-clues and interweavings, set down with full awareness that only the most alert readers will make them conscious.) Freud posited the adult self as riddled with secret chambers not knowable at all, expressing themselves only in dreams, tongue-slips, irrational behaviors, illness. We are psychologically, as biologically, made visible by our desires. Yet display can also conceal, as the raised quills of a porcupine disguise the vulnerability and true size of its actual body. This is the sleight of hand of the sequinned magician, the strategy of the shy person who cultivates the persona of outrageous dress to cover the fear of strangeness with further strangeness.

Revelation as a journey toward an individuated self is described in the myth of Psyche, the girl taken in marriage by Eros after his mother Venus, already jealous of her great beauty, has sent him to do her harm. Fearing his mother's increased anger, Eros keeps the marriage secret and visits Psyche only in darkness, warning her of disaster should she try to discover who he is. (An odd displacement, this, since it is Venus from whom the transgression must be concealed.) Their joyous if half-unconscious arrangement might have continued unbroken, but convinced by jealous sisters that her unseen husband must be a monster, one night Psyche comes with a lamp to the bed where he sleeps. As she stands breathless before his beauty, a drop of hot lamp oil falls onto his shoulder, and the god awakens and flees. In the aftermath of that revelation Psyche's difficult trials of individuation begin – aided throughout, it is worth remembering, by powers that lie outside the scope of both conscious intelligence and intention.

Perhaps one message to be taken from the many myths that speak of a broken concealment is the need for tact. In life, as in literature and myth, the impulse toward a simple stripping down to some bare truth is either delusion, hubris, or the reductionist's dust. As there is a connection between modesty, the generative, and a clear-seeing compassion, there is one also between hubris and blindness. What is bared without sufficient respect may not be bearable, or bearable only at enormous cost. Yet until she engages the world with oil lamp and open eyes, Psyche cannot become what her name has come to mean: a soul, a being engaged in the full living-through of her own deep existence.

At times though, the hidden's job may be to remain fully hidden. A knowledge too definitive can diminish; an alert unknowing keeps open the most broad range of what is possible. Richard Hugo counselled young poets never to ask a question in their poems to which they knew the answer. Chekhov advised his brother, 'Art doesn't provide answers, it can only formulate questions correctly.' Certain jokes, teaching tales, and koans share a similar intention: to dismantle all certainties concerning a person's place in the world.

In one traditional Hasidic story, a man tortured by doubt travels a great distance hoping to ask a famous teacher his question. At first, the teacher's disciples will not allow the stranger into the study house, but one day he finds a way to slip in, approaches the Rebbe, and speaks: 'Venerable Rebbe, forgive me for disturbing you, but I have travelled many weeks and waited many days for the chance to ask you a question that has troubled me all my adult life.' 'What is your question?', the teacher responds. The man asks, 'What is the essence of truth?' The Rebbe looks at his visitor for a moment, rises from his chair, approaches, and slaps him hard. Then he withdraws again to his books. Shocked, the questioner retreats to a tavern across the way, bitterly and loudly complaining of his mistreatment. One of the teacher's disciples, overhearing, takes pity and explains: 'The Rebbe's slap was given you in great kindness, to teach you this: never surrender a good question for a mere answer.'

When the world is looked at from the condition of mind that questions, each thing is seen both for itself as it is and as the holder of the immeasurable secrets good questions unlatch. A world – or a book – felt to contain the hidden is inexhaustible to the imagination, yielding new possibilities to each moment that presents itself as question more than as answer. It is their inability to be known completely that infuses aliveness into good poems – the way they are, as the poet Donald Hall has said, a house with a secret room at its center, the place in which all that cannot be paraphrased is stored. The room can never be opened to ordinary habitation, yet its presence changes the house. And in truth, the unopenable room does not reside in the outward data of the world, or in the words of the poem: it resides in us.

In Islamic imagery, paradise is a walled garden; the Hebrew word from which our English 'Paradise' comes is *Pardes*, whose common meaning is orchard. The Kabbalists map how an orchard becomes the embodied dwelling place of the sacred by showing the hidden meaning that resides in each of its letters. P stands for *peshat*, the mind that sees the world literally; R for *remez*, the understanding of allusion and metonymy; D is for *derash*, metaphoric or symbolic interpretation; and S for *sod* – 'secret'. There is no Paradise, no place of true completion, that does not include within its walls the unknown.

Hiddenness is the ballast in the ship's keel, the great underwater portion of a life that steadies the rest. The thirteenth-century Zen teacher Eihei Dogen described its weight of presence thus: '...there are mountains hidden in treasures. There are mountains hidden in swamps. There are mountains hidden in the sky. There are mountains hidden in mountains. There are mountains hidden in hiddenness. This is complete understanding.'[8]

*

The real is shy of words, and rightly. As Ted Hughes described it, 'Like Cordelia in *King Lear*, perhaps the more sure of itself truth is, the more doubtful it is of the adequacy of words.'[9] Bewilderment before questions of speech and silence, ambivalence before the experience both of seeing and of being seen, run through the words of many writers, including my own. I will close then with two poems by the early twentieth-century Greek poet Cavafy, which speak to the two sides of hiddenness, making a compelling case for each in turn. The first concerns concealment as obstacle and grief. It may emerge from the poet's sexuality, explored in many of his poems though never explicitly named. Still, such an interpretation may well be reductive; the poem may well speak of something even more complexly unsayable. In any case, its reticence on its own subject is inseparable from its meaning.

Hidden Things

From all I did and all I said
let no one try to find out who I was.
An obstacle was there distorting
the actions and the manner of my life.
An obstacle was often there
to stop me when I'd begin to speak.
From my most unnoticed actions,
my most veiled writing –
from these alone will I be understood.
But maybe it isn't worth so much concern,
so much effort to discover who I really am.
Later, in a more perfect society,
someone else made just like me
is certain to appear and act freely.[10]

(tr. by Edmund Keeley and Philip Sherrard)

The second poem, less well-known, has long stayed in my mind as a striking testimony and argument on behalf of hiddenness – for the importance of something done not for the purpose of gaining others' regard but for the sake of the psyche's solitary existence, known neither as subject or object, and for the imagination's own exhilaration in the doing.

For the Shop

He wrapped them up carefully, neatly,
in expensive green silk.

Roses of rubies, lilies of pearl,
violets of amethyst: according to his taste, his will,
his vision of their beauty – not as he saw them in nature
or studied them. He'll leave them in the safe,
examples of his bold, his skillful work.
Whenever a customer comes into the shop,
he brings out other things to sell – first class ornaments:
bracelets, chains, necklaces, rings.[11]

(tr. by Edmund Keeley and Philip Sherrard)

Some may believe that the creation unseen is wasted, its maker selfish. But what I've been trying to examine today is the way that those bold, idiosyncratic jewel-flowers, even concealed, still affect. They change the shop, they change the jeweller, they change even the customer who leaves with his ordinary ring and bracelet. The thought that something we cannot see, of unsurpassable skill and unimaginable form, exists in the back room's locked safe – isn't this, for any artist, for any person, an irresistible hope, beautiful and disturbing as the distant baying of Thoreau's lost hound?

NOTES

1. Michael Dickinson, California Institute of Technology.

2. *Aristotle's Rhetoric and Poetics* (NY: Modern Library, 1954).

3. *New and Collected Poems* by Richard Wilbur (San Diego, NY, and London: Harcourt Brace Jovanovich, 1988).

4. *Transgressions: Selected Poems* by Jack Gilbert (Tarset: Bloodaxe Books, 2006).

5. *Geniuses & Other Eccentrics* by Selden Rodman (San Francisco: Green Trees Press, 1997).

6. 'The Veil of the Soul', in *Marginalia*, published in *The Southern Literary Messenger* in 1849, the last year of Poe's life.

7. *Collected Poems* by W.H. Auden, edited by Edward Mendelson, revised edition (London: Faber and Faber, 2007).

8. Eihei Dogen, *The Mountains and Waters Sutra*, translated by Kazuaki Tanahashi and Arnold Kottler; from *Moon in a Dewdrop*, edited by Kazuaki Tanahashi (Berkeley: North Point Press, 1985).

9. *Winter Pollen* by Ted Hughes (New York: Picador, USA 1995).

10. C.P. Cavafy: *Collected Poems*, translated by Edmund Keeley & Philip Sherrard (Princeton: Princeton University Press, 1975).

11. C.P. Cavafy: *Collected Poems*.

Poetry and Uncertainty

Hesiod called the god Chaos the progenitor of all other beings and things – gods, animals, humans, rocks, stars, waters, vegetation, winds. Existence, it seems, takes root in ground so unfathomable it can only be named and left behind. In one place, the name given is Chaos, in another, the Big Bang. In one well-known story, the name is 'turtles'. The story comes, appropriately, in differing versions. An astronomer, or a physicist, or a philosopher has just finished lecturing on the structure of the cosmos. When he asks for questions, an old woman raises her hand. 'Professor James,' she says – or Russell, or Sagan, or Dyson – 'you are quite an interesting young man, but you've got it all wrong. Everyone knows the universe rests on the back of a very large tortoise.' The speaker answers gently, 'And what does the tortoise rest on?' The woman replies, 'Oh, clever, young man, very clever – but it's turtles all the way down.'

One of the penalties of consciousness is waking each day into the awareness that the future cannot be predicted, that the universe rests on the back of an incomprehensible mystery, that bewilderment, caprice, and the unknowable are among the most faithful companions of any life. Mostly, it seems, we go on by inventing a story. Yet no story completely suffices – eventually the turtle appears, munching its contemplative bit of lettuce.

For those willing to let themselves feel it, any story leaves behind an uneasiness, sometimes at the center, other times at the edge of perception, and like the remainder left over in a problem in long division, it must be carried. Literature's work, in part, and particularly poetry's, is to take up that residue and remnant, to find a way to live amid and alongside the uncertain. Plato banished poets from his republic because he thought poetry escapist, dulling the search for truth by substituting for it the hypnosis of beauty. But good poetry doesn't in fact allay anxiety with answers – it startles its reader out of the general trance, awakening an enlarged reality by means of a close-paid attention to its own ground.

Keats described poetry's relationship to the unknown in a letter he wrote on the winter solstice of 1817. In it he famously ascribed poetic genius to a kind of anti-talent. 'Negative Capability,' he called it, and explained, 'that is when man is capable of being in uncertainties, Mysteries, doubts, without any irritable reaching after fact & reason.' A century later, William Empson echoed Keats's insight when he named ambiguity the central quality of poetic beauty.

Awareness of the fallibility of intention and hope; a steady dose of doubt and self-doubt; knowledge of the Heisenbergian effects of the observer's own existence – these identifiers of human consciousness are also markers for what we call "literature", as opposed to those forms of writing that inform, dictate, plead, or simplistically entertain. Awareness of uncertainty signals the entrance of human individuality into the consciousness of the commons. What we think of as "art" goes further: it makes of our encounter with the uncertain a thing to be sought. Death-fear is turned into *Gilgamesh*, doubt of other and self becomes *Hamlet*, and the relationship to what cannot be known is permanently changed. That anxiety, grief, and the fear of chaos can be turned into beauty, meaning, and the irrefutable pleasure transmutation itself brings, is no small part of literature's mysterious power, whether experienced as Aristotelian catharsis or in more subtle forms.

Knowing and not-knowing, uncertainty and certainty, were much on Keats's mind during that early nineteenth-century winter. A month earlier, he wrote in another letter, 'I am certain of nothing but the heart's affections and the truth of imagination – what the imagination seizes as beauty must be truth – whether it existed before or not.' By mid-January, he wrote: 'There's nothing stable in the world – uproar's your only music.' The preceding century's Enlightenment confidence in rationality and control has been thoroughly discarded, yet the paralysis of Shakespeare's Danish prince is nowhere to be found. In place of objective knowledge and permanence, Keats puts his faith in the chameleon interior life: quick on its feet, subjective, supple, eager to be seized by the ground it finds itself on. (If Hamlet had had the Negative Capability of his creator, he might have lived to become the fine king Fortinbras declares he could have been.)

To exchange certainty for praise of mystery and doubt is to step back from hubris and stand in the receptive, both vulnerable and exposed. The Heian-era Japanese poet Izumi Shikibu expressed a similar understanding in one of her tanka. Written around the year 1000, its thirty-one syllables – in the original Japanese – agree to, even invite, Keats's instability and 'uproar':

It is true,
the wind blows terribly here –
but moonlight
also leaks between the roof planks
of this ruined house.[1]

(tr. by Jane Hirshfield and Mariko Aratani)

Shikibu's poem reminds its reader that beauty, and also the Buddhist awakening frequently signalled in Japanese poetry by the image of moonlight, will come to a person only if the full range of events and feelings are allowed into his or her life. Real permeability cannot be provisional. It is impossible to know what will enter if the house of the solidified and defended self is breached, and ruin is not a condition any person willingly seeks. Still, those gaps in the roof planks – not the assigned doors, the expected windows – are the opening through which the luminous arrives.

We tend to think of good poems as preserving and transmitting some knowledge, often hard won. And, as with Shikibu's tanka, they do. Still, more often than not, poetry comes into being as response to the fracture of knowing and sureness – from not understanding, yet still meeting whatever arrives. The person who searches for answers will be a person assailed by questions; the biographies of poets, like those of mystics, are filled with dark nights of the soul. The Polish poet Anna Swirszczynska ('Anna Swir') described that bleakness directly, but also with a certain detachment, even good humor:

Poetry Reading

I'm curled into a ball
like a dog
that is cold.

Who will tell me
why I was born,
why this monstrosity
called life.

The telephone rings. I have to give
a poetry reading.

I enter.
A hundred people, a hundred pairs of eyes.
They look, they wait.
I know for what.

I am supposed to tell them
why they were born,
why there is
this monstrosity called life.[2]

(tr. by Czeslaw Miłosz and Leonard Nathan)

Poetry often enacts a recovering of wholeness, of emotional and metaphysical balance, whether in an individual (the lyric poem's task) or in a culture (the task of the epic). Yet to do that work, a poem needs to retain within itself some of the disequilibrium that called it forth, and also to include the uncomfortable remainder, the undissolvable residue carried over – that inclusiveness is what wholeness means. Anna Swirszczynska's poem is virtually all remainder. It refuses any idealisation of poetic wisdom, any transformative lyric closure; it ends as it begins. Yet still this poem does what good poems do: it increases our sense of being fully human. It counters isolation and meaninglessness, even while seeming to offer no replacement. The satisfaction this poem gives its reader – and for me, Swirszczynska's poem does bring a considerable solace – comes in its reminder of the commonality of grief, perplexity, and the failure to comprehend or transcend. By borrowing what is so often the strategy of comedy – that is, by admitting the truth – the poem makes despair more bearable just by showing it is what it is: a touchstone of any life spent without blinders.

Izumi Shikibu's tanka is not so different from this as it may first seem – if the reader doesn't grant the wind and leaking house their full, ongoing severity, the poem's moonlight means nothing. The relationship between uncertainty and solace in these poems – as in life – is not curative; it is one of "also". And that is enough. Wallace Stevens felt writing an act of self-preservation, the imagination pressing back against the pressure of the real. This describes less a wisdom coolly achieved than some sleight of hand or aikido gesture worked by language. The most serene works on the bookshelf are nonetheless in the lineage of Scheherezade's stories – art holding incoherence and death at bay with the changing shapes of beauty, ingenuity, and suspense. This is Sartre's definition of genius: not a gift, but the escape a person invents in desperate times.

Fear makes good ground for literature, it seems. The earliest recorded writing for which we know a historical author is Enheduanna's 'Hymn to Inanna'; the occasion of its composition was an act of savagery during a Sumerian war. Over four millennia later, Virginia Woolf alluded to poetry's role during similar times. In *To the Lighthouse*'s center section, Woolf describes the effects of time on the Ramsays' summer cottage in the Hebrides – a house, like Izumi Shikibu's, going to ruin. Unvisited, untended, its wallpaper loosens; a shawl draped over a mounted boar's head comes free, corner by corner, over years; window frames, plaster, and roof shingles yield to the elements. In brief, bracket-held sentences, a series of revelations appear, each a small telegram interrupting the house's gradual fall into decay – the eldest son, Andrew, is blown up by a shell on the fields of the Great War; the daughter Prue weds and then dies giving birth; Woolf slips the death of Mrs Ramsay herself into a passing phrase. A more casual bit of information also appears: the Ramsays' house-guest poet August Carmichael has become an unexpected success. The novel explains it thus: 'The war, people said, had revived their interest in poetry.'

A lyric poem does not solve any outward dilemma; few answer any practical question, none refastens a single shingle to a house. As Auden wrote in his elegy for Yeats, 'poetry makes nothing happen'. Yet when crisis requires a mode of negotiation with the chaos, entropy, and loss-terror that are the steady co-inhabitors of human life, poems are turned toward, as a plant requiring light turns toward the sun.

How to name where poetry's consoling powers may lie? One part can be found in what has already been seen in Anna Swir-szczynska's poem, the sense of connection with others that good poems both emerge from and forge. In entering the imaginative, metaphoric, or narrative expression of another, even if it is the expression of pain, longing, or fear, you find yourself less lonely, accompanied in this life. Another part may come in what the medieval alchemists called *solutio* – the process of making some-thing workable and transformable by making it more fluid, whether in the physical or metaphysical realms. A difficult thing is 'hard', we say; a mathematical answer arrived at is 'solved'. A good poem, then, is a solvent, a kind of WD-40 for the soul. This is the efficacy of Aristotle's catharsis. Simply to feel oneself moved creates an increase of freedom; outward circumstance is not the self's only definition when the imagination presses back against it. Primo Levi described the exhilaration he felt at Auschwitz, when, sent with a fellow prisoner to fetch the midday soup, he attempted to reconstruct and recite for his friend (with whom he could scarcely communicate, not sharing a language) a canto from Dante. During those minutes, each recovered in himself what it was to feel fully human.

Yet another part of poetry's solace, related to *solutio*, is the increase of subtlety a good poem provides. Subtlety's etymological roots rest in loom-woven cloth. It is the name we give to thought that is both finely textured and free of range, able to connect disparate qualities into the unified, usable fabric of a new whole. Respect of the uncertain is subtlety's inscape. In subtle response, thought is stitched into place with its own undertows, opposites and extensions, with a mind that questions and crosshatches its statements and feelings. Language itself is subtle by nature, multi-stranded of meaning – and what is good poetry if not language awake to its own powers? Even in poems that may seem to risk the didactic, the buoying tact of the particular – whether in images, metaphors, music, or rhetoric – counter-balances certitude's arrogance and leaden pull. The recognition of language's skillful means extends far beyond literature. 'Style,' the nuclear physicist J. Robert Oppenheimer once said, 'is the deference action pays to uncertainty. It is above all style through which power defers to reason.'

Subtle thinking liberates its subject from the expected and assumed, from ordinary versions of what is thought true. On the scales of exact/inexact, accurate/inaccurate, right/wrong, true/false, subtlety steps to the side, slicing through such categories as Chuang-tzu's Taoist butcher sliced through the bones of the ox – where the joints fall open. Yet to find the places of openness is not to be vague. Another exchange that followed a physicist's lecture comes to mind, this one involving Nils Bohr. Bohr had spoken on complementarity, and one listener thought to ask him what the complement of objective truth ('*Wirklichkeit*') might be. 'Clarity,' he replied.

Clarity is factuality that looks and feels more widely, letting in more than it knows it knows. It is as good a name as we may find for the combination of attentiveness, accuracy, and permeability to subtlety's undertone and shadow that we recognise in good poems. Some poems cannot be parsed at all, yet we still recognise them as consummately clear. The difference between clarity and objectively graspable fact is the difference between a live blue Morpho and one pinned for display. The dead butterfly's beauty is precisely what it was, yet even a black and white sumi ink sketch, in which almost everything is left out, might hold more of the original vibrance.[3]

Whitman points toward the quality of clear-seeing in another way, when he contrasts a narrow academic perception, caught up in only its own knowledge and numbers, with the way of looking – in the phrase 'from time to time', it seems almost bashful – of the 'unaccountable' self:

When I Heard the Learned Astronomer

When I heard the learn'd astronomer,
When the proofs, the figures, were ranged in columns before me,
When I was shown the charts and diagrams, to add, divide, and
     measure them,
When I sitting heard the astronomer where he lectured with much
     applause in the lecture room,

How soon unaccountable I became tired and sick,
Till rising and gliding out I wander'd off by myself,
In the mystical moist night-air, and from time to time,
Look'd up in perfect silence at the stars.

It is in subtle ways that a good poem is able both to answer
uncertainty and contain it. Here is an early poem by Czesław
Miłosz, written in 1936 in Wilno, now Vilnius, in Lithuania.
Nothing in it overtly resembles Whitman's poem, yet it offers
its reader an experience recognisably the same – an enlargement
of being, the slowed and deepened breath that comes with the
release of fixed ideas for the more complex real.

Encounter

We were riding through frozen fields in a wagon at dawn.
A red wing rose in the darkness.

And suddenly a hare ran across the road.
One of us pointed to it with his hand.

That was long ago. Today neither of them is alive,
Not the hare, nor the man who made the gesture.

O my love, where are they, where are they going,
The flash of a hand, streak of movement, rustle of pebble.
I ask, not out of sorrow, but in wonder.[4]

(tr. by Czeslaw Miłosz and Lillian Vallee)

The poem transcribes bird, hare, a pointing hand, and through
them, the brutality that is transience. For resolution, it offers
nothing beyond Miłosz's characteristic gesture of rescue: memory.
There is no solving the central dilemma: time strips the world
of all we have known and seen, and the knower and seer will
not be exempt. And still, this small lyric carries large solace;
respecting the ground of uncertainty by being one part answer,
one part question, one part thrown open window. Its 'answer' may
be described as its honoring of particularity and remembrance;
its question is overt ('O my love, where are they, where are they
going'); and the window – which must escape precise description,
being opening rather than presence – might be the way that a
landscape of frozen winter fields and a diction of plain reportage
somehow become, in the turn towards invocation, a tenderness

surpassing ordinary grief, ordinary loss. This poem doesn't diminish time's losses by simple protest – it is instead a wagon travelling outside the ego's domain, like Whitman stepping outside the lecture hall to the hall of true stars.

*

The making of good poetry entails control; it also requires surrender and a light hand. A genuine art lives somewhere between the divination bones and the dice. That is, it lives along that exploration line that has to do with which aspects of our lives we can know, which we cannot, and the spirit and tools with which we engage the question. We travel this line by taking aim with a whole life, and then letting go, committing ourselves to the toss.

Some early divination bones and certain early dice (according to magician and historian of magic Ricky Jay, some die found in Egyptian tombs 6,000 years old may have already been loaded) were both made of astragali – the squarish heel bones of hoofed animals, especially antelopes and sheep. But the role these two play in the psyche is not the same. Divination, however mistaken, is the beginning of science: a tool for experimental observation, the thrown bones searched for a verifiably predictable world.[5] But gamblers' dice do not search for a path toward the knowable, they are a reply tossed gamely – in both that word's senses – into the face of the uncertain. The terrain of dice is feeling, not truth. Faced with what cannot be known, the gambler's response is to take it on. Spinning the wheel, wagering, playing the odds, we engage the unengagable and hope to win.

Gaming courts the experience of uncertainty as much as it contains it. This is true of poems as well. Luck and inspiration are siblings, if not twins. Luck – the name we give to chance's mysterious counterweight – is a state of grace we feel to be turning the dice in our favor. The smile of the Muse feels the same. Inspiration comes and goes on its own currents and whim. True, a cluster of good dice-falls – if the die are honest – is simply the laws of probability having their way. But inside the psyche, that phenomenon has its own resonance. The neurophysiology of decision-making reveals that the higher the uncertainty of an experience, the greater the dopamine pleasure-response in the brain on its successful resolution.[6] No surprise then that every culture has developed the taste for gambling. An optimistic relationship to the unknown and the random is evolutionarily useful – whether in hunting a meal or a mate, resilience in the face of delay and uncertainty is required.

The encounter with the unknown is a nutrient in life, as essential as certain vitamins – without it, the soul falls into sleep, depression and despair. The trick then is how much, and when, to admit the random, chaotic, unknowable, into our lives. It is always a matter of balance. The child at the mercy of an incomprehensible world requires reassurance; the adult, stalled in the familiar, may require an opposite prod. As will be explored more fully in the third of these essays, it is in the encounter with the unexpected and the uncertain that both learning and strong emotion occur – in a situation where nothing is new or changed, the repertory of experience will be confirmed, but not expanded. Whether in art or in science, the periphery of the already known is where richness and transformation lie, whether the renovation is of thought, feeling, or technique. Too much familiarity asks no attention; too much that is new cannot be comprehended at all.

The pleasure of a pursuit made without guarantee allows a writer or painter to persevere, even if externally unrewarded for years: the wagered hope, the adrenaline-risk of failure, are themselves part of the lure. Any artist seeking a true discovery, like any person seeking an unplacid life, must be willing to stand in harm's way – behind the door there may be a lady, or there may be a tiger. A story by Jorge Luis Borges, lover of tigers, sketches the attraction of deliberately courted chance. The narrator of 'The Lottery in Babylon' describes a society in which a lottery has expanded from its usual form to govern every aspect of life, subjecting a person to potential impoverishment as much as potential prosperity, and affecting societal role along with financial status, so that a person might go from proconsul to slave to thief to priest as the drawing of the lots decrees. The result – since The Company in charge of the lottery functions invisibly – is a world exactly like our own, but compressed, steepened, 'saturated', as the narrator puts it, 'with chance'. 'I

35

have known,' he says, 'what the Greeks do not know, incertitude' – a sentence set down with pride. Those who think the Company fictitious are branded heretic, and fools: for Borges's imagined Babylonians, a world believed governed by secret drawings is more alive than one which is not. To feel is to be at risk, and to be at risk is to feel.

Like an animal hunted as much for the challenge as for the meat or pelt, artistic masterpieces come into the world as a mix: part talent, part effort, part training, part cultural context – but also part inspiration, part luck, part the love of taking a chance. Change is saturated with chance in all its phases. From an asteroid collision to errors in genetic transcription, evolution is driven by accident, mishap, mistake. Transcription errors have their way in poems as well. Every writer has experienced the intention to set down one word, but then accidentally writing another, recognised instantly as better – more accurate, more surprising. Composing in rhyme and meter is throwing the word-dice in exactly that hope. A statement is made without knowing where it will lead, and the end word of the line must then summon from the pool of all possible words one similar to itself, yet not perfectly so. Through the play of imperfect replication, thought – like biological life – evolves in unexpected directions: uncertainty both courted and contained. The process extends even to typographical error. Malcolm Lowry, though more commonly remembered for his novels, wrote a small and perfect poem on this phenomenon, which, fittingly, turned out to be the last work of his life:

Strange Type

I wrote 'in the dark cavern of our birth'.
The printer had it tavern, which seems better.
But herein lies the subject of our mirth,
Since on the next page death appears as dearth.
So it may be that God's word was distraction,
Which to our strange type appears destruction,
Which is bitter.[7]

Poems, if they are any good at all, hold a knowledge elusive and multiple, unsayable in any other form. Resonant, fragrant, travelling more than one direction at a time, poetic speech escapes narrowing abstraction and reification as richly as does life itself. This is why lyric poems are so rife, as Lowry's is, with irony – good poems undercut their own yearning to say one thing well, because to say one thing is simply not to say enough. Too much certainty and single-mindedness irritates as well as bores; the idea that one can know what is right, or that a general truth is possible, is an insult to the real. The Portuguese poet Fernando Pessoa captured this in one of the small, perfect poems he wrote in the persona of Alberto Caeiro:

They Spoke to Me of People, and of Humanity

They spoke to me of people, and of humanity.
But I've never seen people, or humanity.
I've seen various people, astonishingly dissimilar,
Each separated from the next by an unpeopled space.[8]

(tr. by Richard Zenith)

Each time I read this poem, I feel an enormous relief. It is Whitman walking out of the lecture hall, or Yehuda Amichai's more contemporary version of the same impulse:

A Great Tranquillity: Questions and Answers

The people in the painfully bright auditorium
spoke about religion
in the life of contemporary man
and about God's place in it.

People spoke in excited voices
as they do at airports.
I walked away from them:
I opened an iron door marked 'Emergency'
and entered into
a great tranquillity: Questions and Answers.[9]

(tr. by Chana Bloch)

*

How then does poetry speak with an appropriate humility and tact, in a world where certainty appears increasingly a threat to both humanity's and the planet's continuance? How accurately respect a world in which each second requires a new and particular question, even as it answers the last moment's query? There are, I suspect, four basic strategies. One is Malcolm Lowry's alternative to destruction – distraction. We might at first think this an act of denial – a kind of whistling in the dark – but more kindly and fully, it is the choice to survive; to live "as if", and go on with the large and small affairs of a life, its loves, labors, and the ordinary pleasures of clean sheets and slow-cooked soup. This strategy is the difference between a Dutch *vanitas* painting, with its overt, contemplative skull, and the painted landscape showing a bustling town, a harvest scene, a winter pond thick with skaters. Whatever lies under the latter's ice, joy is above it. As in the daily conduct of a life itself, moment by moment, the greatest portion of poems fall into this class. They do not concern themselves with certainty or uncertainty, their business is elsewhere. Yet they bow toward uncertainty's directives, as all good art does: they do not over-insist, their beauty is made in ambiguity, their windows are open, their skaters glide in the company of their own shadows.

A second strategy is directness, an open-eyed acceptance – to make one's peace with things as they are and love the world as transient, as frail. This is the approach that found such a powerful response in the poem by Adam Zagajewski that ran in the *New Yorker* following the events of September 11, 2001. 'Try to praise the mutilated world,' it began. 'Remember June's long days, the wild strawberries, drops of wine, the dew. The nettles that methodically overgrow / the abandoned homesteads of exiles.' Zagajewski's images' fragile tenderness in the midst of destruction were precisely the medicine needed in those stunned days, antidote to both fundamentalism and fear.

A short lyric by the Roman poet Horace provides an earlier poetic model for this stance of straightforward, unsimplifying acceptance:

I, 11

Leucon, no one's allowed to know his fate,
Not you, not me: don't ask, don't hunt for answers
In tea leaves or palms. Be patient with whatever comes.
This could be our last winter, it could be many

More, pounding the Tuscan Sea on these rocks:
Do what you must, be wise, cut your vines
And forget about hope. Time goes running, even
As we talk. Take the present, the future's no one's affair.[10]

(tr. by Burton Raffel)

It's worth noticing that the strategy of directness is also to be found in those children's books that endure in the mind for a lifetime. E.B. White's *Charlotte's Web* introduces a child both to the fearful concept of death and to a means toward death's accommodation. There is no pretense of superheroic immortality, no fantasy of permanent escape. The young pig Wilbur will someday die, as does his protector in the book, the spider Charlotte. But the knowledge of cycles is given, the presence of beloved companions, and the provision that verve, affection, and a generous imagination do matter, do clear, within transience, the preserving space in which a life can take place.

The third strategy, already glimpsed in Izumi Shikibu's tanka, is to make of uncertainty a home. It can be thought of as standing out in the rain so long that, soaked through, one grows once again warm; or if not warm, drenched to the point there is no reason left to seek shelter. Numerous contemporary poets work deeply the indeterminacy of meaning. But in this mode of meeting uncertainty's dilemma, the most heartbreaking practitioner is Paul Celan, whose post-Holocaust poems, written in what he felt as the language of death – his home tongue of German – fracture their own words almost past speaking. Celan described himself as possessing a 'true-stammered mouth', the world as a thing 'to be stuttered after'.

NO MORE SAND ART, no sand book, no masters.
Nothing on the dice. How many mutes?
Seventeen.

Your question – your answer.
Your song, what does it know?
Deepinsnow,
Eepinnow,
E-i-o.[11]

(tr. by John Felstiner)

The poem – entirely uncertainty, except for the enigmatically precise 'seventeen' – erases itself from existence; yet that erasure is itself so powerful as to be permanently engraved. John Felstiner, the poem's translator, has assembled critical speculation on some of the associative meanings – the seventeen mutes might be 'eighteen minus one', significant because in Hebrew numerology, eighteen spells 'alive'. No special knowledge is needed to feel the resonance of those unmarked dice, or of the final phrase's burial in its own enactment – but it chills to be reminded that words which in German are reduced only to their vowels are in Hebrew words that would no longer exist. In the life, as is well known, the silence won – Celan committed suicide in 1970, at age 49. But biography and art are not identical, and the poems remain, each an adamant refusal both of certainty's easy speaking and of silence.

It may be that all good poems attempt to find the refuge of what can be said without betraying uncertainty's abiding presence. Striking that lit-match balance is how poetry approaches our sense of the experienced real, which is equally wavering, fragile, subject to sudden changes of wind. In one poem the solution might appear as spiritual amplitude tempered by mystery and shadow, in another it takes the turn toward what is absolutely basic and spare. This, I believe, is the fourth strategy: a faithful reporting of only that which is present. Knowing nothing, a person can look to see what is here: ten fingers, ten toes, the experience of breathing, a chair. Pessoa wrote many such poems, in which he tried to strip ideas away from the real. Most, like the one given earlier, address that concept abstractly; a few provide small demonstrations of what it might be like to live in such a manner:

This May Be the Last Day of My Life

This may be the last day of my life.
I lifted my right hand to wave at the sun,
But I did not wave at it in farewell.
I was glad I could still see it – that's all.[12]

(tr. by Richard Zenith)

'The Fly', by the Czech poet and immunologist Miroslav

Holub, is also a poem of a simply recorded, imagined present. It addresses itself to uncertainty with indirect but unexpected force – as any honest describing of what happens (perhaps necessarily?) must:

The Fly

She sat on a willow-trunk
watching
part of the battle of Crécy,
the shouts,
the gasps,
the groans,
the tramping and the tumbling.

During the fourteenth charge
of the French cavalry
she mated
with a brown-eyed male fly
from Vadincourt.

She rubbed her legs together
as she sat on a disembowelled horse
meditating
on the immortality of flies.

With relief she alighted
on the blue tongue
of the Duke of Clervaux.

When silence settled
and only the whisper of decay
softly circled the bodies

and only
a few arms and legs
still twitched jerkily under the trees,

she began to lay her eggs
on the single eye
of Johann Uhr,
the Royal Armourer.

And thus it was
that she was eaten by a swift
fleeing
from the fires of Estrées.[13]

(tr. by George Theiner)

A friend whose current research investigates decision-making in flies wrote in a recent letter:

> I think the magnitude of uncertainly, U, is expressed well mathematically, as:
>
> $$U = abs\,(\ I\ /\ (C\text{-}B)\ )$$
>
> where I is the perceived impact of a decision, estimates C and B are the cost and benefits of the decision, and *abs* denotes absolute value (angst over things we decide to do is just as painful as angst over things we decide not to do). The direct relationship with impact is reasonably clear – we generally don't sweat the stuff that doesn't matter. Door number one or door number three: big impact. The lady or the tiger: big impact. 'Would you like fresh cracked pepper?': little impact. The denominator is much more interesting; uncertainty "blows up" when the difference between our notions of the costs and benefits of any given action are small. Chinese menus are tough because so many items are nearly identical. Our struggles with ordering from menus illustrate well the nuances of uncertainty. I haven't eaten at McDonalds in a while, but I don't remember great mental turmoil choosing a Big Mac over a Quarter Pounder with cheese. Although the cost and benefits are nearly identical, the impact is very low. But my brain disassembles when trying to choose an appetiser at Chez Panisse. There is a finite chance that this could be the most wonderful thing I will ever eat and I don't want to miss that opportunity.
>
> As for insects, they may not think but they certainly make lots of decisions. What we perceive as behavior is really just a seamless string of decisions: should I mate with you?, should I vomit here?, should I fly off this overcrowded rotting peach on the chance I'll find a lovely uninhabited rotting peach? Flies make decisions forcefully, uninhibited by memory and nostalgia. Little six-legged Fortinbras. We like Hamlet better, because his uncertainty cuts so close to the source of our humanity. We cannot tabulate costs and benefits without being helplessly swayed by our memories and emotions. We get all bollixed up with uncertainty because we really don't see things clearly. Our minds drift and we can't quite manage to pull the trigger. Not like Arnold the Terminator's '*Hasta la vista*, baby'. Soldiers, the humans specifically trained to face the most wrenching of all decisions, must learn to act with the emotionless certainty of flies and robots.[14]

My friend was not responding directly to Holub's poem – I'd asked him only for his thoughts on uncertainty in general, given his research. Still, his inadvertent gloss on its contents points straight to the poem's rhetorical success. By keeping his vision on the fly at its center, Holub presents the human dimension of the scene the more bitterly clearly. What is left unmentioned in that landscape shouts back from past the poem's edge. And that it is left unmentioned is one aspect of how uncertainty inhabits all poems, woven into their fabric in a way virtually structurally required – if a work is the interweaving of complex and multiple parts, it must be held up by its places of openness as much as by its points of connection. Inside that unspeaking openness, some large part of a poem's work takes place – completed not on the page, but inside the writer's or reader's own fullness of being. Words on the page neither ponder nor grieve – what lives in a poem lives in us.

What I have been saying here at such great length is rather simple – to be human is to be unsure, and if the purpose of poetry is to deepen the humanness in us, poetry will be unsure as well. By the navigation of open-ended yet resonant conclusions, by multifaceted statement, by subtle resolutions and non-resolutions of circumstance and sound, good poetry helps us be more richly uncertain, in more profound ways. St Augustine said of Time, 'If you don't ask me what Time is, I know, but if you ask what it is, then I don't.' The more I've thought about uncertainty in poems, the more I've come to appreciate his words. But the truth is, we don't need to understand uncertainty or time for them to accomplish their work in our lives, or in poems – all we need do is live them out and through, and that, well, that can scarcely be avoided.

NOTES

1. *The Ink Dark Moon: Love Poems by Ono no Komachi and Izumi Shikibu, Women of the Ancient Court of Japan* (New York: Vintage Classics, 1990).

2. *Talking to My Body* by Anna Swir (Port Townsend, WA: Copper Canyon Press, 1996).

3. A directly opposite interpretation of this interchange is equally plausible, one in which Bohr's point would have been that reality is too complex to be captured by any understanding that could be experienced as clarity. Each reading of the dialogue holds its appeal; that both are possible illustrates uncertainty's largesse.

4. *New and Collected Poems* by Czeslaw Miłosz (New York: The Ecco Press, 2001).

5. The bones stand at the beginning of writing as well – in the mythological pantheon of China, as in Plato's Greece, the patron god of divination is the god who also brings writing into the world. Among the earliest abstract markings are those notched onto bones; such artifacts go back at least 15,000, and possibly 40,000 years. To imagine the moment of discovery is easy: on an about-to-be discarded femur or rib, someone notices the marks of the hunting axe, a row of nicks and scrapings left by the flaked-stone knife. Bone, whose hardened structure enables terrestrial fleetness, is transformed, after death, into something quite different: a way to make a record at once portable and lasting. It is a first glimmering intimation of paper.

6. Dr Gregory Berns, Emory University (Atlanta, Georgia).

7. *The Collected Poetry of Malcolm Lowry*, edited by Kathleen Scherf (Vancouver: University of British Columbia Press, 1992).

8. *Fernando Pessoa & Co.: Selected Poems*, translated by Richard Zenith (New York: Grove Press, 1998).

9. *The Selected Poetry of Yehuda Amichai*, revised and expanded edition, translated by Chana Bloch and Stephen Mitchell (Berkeley and Los Angeles: University of California Press, 1996).

10. *The Essential Horace*, translated by Burton Raffel (San Francisco: North Point Press, 1983).

11. *Paul Celan: Poet, Survivor, Jew* by John Felstiner (New Haven: Yale University Press, 1995).

12. *Fernando Pessoa & Co.: Selected Poems*, translated by Richard Zenith (New York: Grove Press, 1998).

13. *Poems Before & After: Collected English Translations* by Miroslav Holub, various translators, second edition (Tarset: Bloodaxe Books, 2006).

14. Michael Dickinson, California Institute of Technology (Pasadena, California, USA).

Poetry and the Constellation of Surprise

Each instant of a good poem provides the enactment of an un-fathomable transformation. From the silence preceding the title's first word to that first word, from the first word to the second, everything is changed. The illimitable possibility of the empty page becomes one particular constellation of feeling, thought, interior shift, and musical gesture: the many-levelled experience we feel as "meaning". A good poem makes self and world knowable in new ways, brings us into an existence opened, augmented, and altered. Part of its work, then, must also be to surprise – to awaken into new circumference is to be startled.

Poems that last transport us into previously unanticipatable comprehensions. In this, lyric epiphany is like any learning sharply won: its surprise is the signal of strongly shifted knowledge. But one of the distinguishing powers of art is that it un-seals its experience freshly not only once, but many times. Good poems provide an informing so simultaneously necessary and elusive that they are never, it seems, taken in fully, and can never be fully used up. New each time they are read, good poems offer a kind of mirror-opposite to Tantalus's Hell – each time we enter poetry's realm, we find hunger both wholly present and wholly answered.

It is the mystery of poetry's perennial freshness this essay sets out to explore – what is it that preserves a great poem's power to move its readers each time as if new? Other conceptual realms are not like this. Even discoveries so revolutionary as those made by Copernicus, Kepler and Newton eventually become taken for granted: impersonal, emotionally neutral, as calm and fixed in the mental landscape as a long-familiar chair or backyard boulder. These things may – and do – still astonish, if contemplated closely. Still, their usefulness does not depend on the strength and depth of our reaction to their existence. In art, the response is the actual discovery – whether conceptual, aesthetic or emotional, whether consciously parsed or felt as uncomprehendingly as an ox feels the stick. A poem long memorised can raise in its holder, mid-saying, stunned revelation. Ezra Pound put it simply, 'Poetry is news that stays news.'

It is, of course, we who house poems as much as their words, and we ourselves must be the locus of poetry's depth of newness. Still, the permeability seems to travel both ways: a changed self will find new meanings in a good poem, but a good poem also changes the shape of the self. Having read it, we are not who we were the moment before. Awareness matters if this reciprocity is to happen, and art's first seduction is the summoning and instigation of presence. If a poem, piano concerto, or painting does not feel alive and pressing, demanding from us the attention of current discovery, it is not, at that moment, fully art – only something travelling under art's name with which we happen to share a room. A work of art is not color knifed or brushed onto a canvas, not shaped rock or fired clay, a vibrating cello string, black ink on a page – it is our active, agile, and participatory collaboration with those forms, colors, symbols and sounds. Art lives in what it awakens in us.

Transformation itself carries meaning. The feeling of passage undertaken and alteration undergone is foundation rock for an inhabited, first-hand existence. If art is constructed experience aspiring to the weight of the real, one touchstone of what we feel real, rather than imagined, is this sense of transitive physicality: of our own embodied, altering, and participatory presence. Outward dimensionality is seen by physically shifting the eye; a parallel experience holds for the psyche. A life felt as full is full of change. Describing the experience of emotion, we call ourselves "moved". In biological life, transformation is an unnegotiable given. In art, it is the hallmark struck into a work that works.

Poems preserve their inaugural newness in part because they are like the emotions – not object, but experience, event. The emotions must always be primal, because they are local and unextractable, occurring only in present-time: emotion informs of current circumstance, current needs. Poems that matter – and last – are those that do not lose the power to astonish and move their readers in equally immediate ways. The same poem that resists time's erasure also lives in and by it. It is the score to a music in which the reader is instrument and audience both: not conclusion or summation, but an orchestration of self whose meaning cannot be named except by being played again fully through.

Poetic realisation is evaporative, volatile: while the poem can hold it stably, memory cannot. Like certain chemical, or perhaps alchemical, reactions, a poem is held in the vessel and procedures of its own making. Even the mind of the author cannot seem to keep what has been found: great poems exceed their creators. They are more capacious, compassionate, original, witty, strange, avaricious for range and beauty; their surprises are, as the etymology of the word 'surprise' literally states, beyond grasp. This is why the biographies of poets often puzzle. The life neither fully accounts for nor reflects the poems' achievement. There is no explanation for a Larkin or Dickinson, but also not for Celan, Blake, Hopkins, Whitman or Shakespeare. Neither the narrative arc of the personal nor the historical times nor their intersection can precipitate the art. The creative leap is inconceivable until it is done – not least because a certain inconceivability is part of its nature. Lyric epiphany, it seems, gives off a kind of protective mist or exudate, an amnesia to any generalisable recall. And what can't be remembered will (re)appear to us as new.

Creative discoveries are made by generative re-combination: disparate elements brought together in a way not previously seen, then recognised as making a useful whole. Cognition begins with the construction and distinction of patterns. From the infant's 'buzzing and blooming confusion', in William James's phrase, we assemble a comprehensible world by perceiving first what stays or recurs. Only then can we see the alterations, which combinations are new and can newly inform. The greater the distance and leap of effective connection, the more surprise it will hold; the most profound discoveries – those described as revolutionary or "earth-shaking" – are ones, like the Copernican rearrangement of sun and planets, that revise our most daily, unquestioned assumptions. The Latin verb *cogitare*, 'to think', has its roots in the act of shaking things together – agitation of the existing order is needed to make something new, a principle contained in trickster myths and social revolutions worldwide. Intelligence is a little different. The Latin *intelligo* refers to sorting and intentional selection. This reminds of Chekhov's definition of talent: the ability to tell the essential and inessential apart.

If the mind recognises discovery by its perception of change and the unexpected, any creativity that matters, then, must surprise. Surprise erases the known for the new. Counterfactual thought's "what if " resides on a spectrum; play also shakes things together – often quite literally – in new ways. But while the results of play both instruct of the world and bring pleasure, they rarely jolt. Make-believe plays its indispensable role in a life precisely because it doesn't "count": it is experience undertaken without the commitment of outer-world repercussion. The distinction clarifies why some poems seem essential, while others, as accomplished and interesting of surface, do not. Deep surprise is the way the mind signals itself that a thing perceived or thought is consequential, that a discovery may be of actual use. (The experience itself, though, especially in responding to a work of art, may well be felt as some different emotion, the one that follows; surprise itself, neuroscientists report, lasts half a second at most.) We can think of the role of surprise in survival's own sorting – what most surprises will be most strongly acted on, and most strongly learned. The poems we carry forward, as individuals and as cultures, are those that not only strike us powerfully but also hold some reason to call up their own recall. They are the poems we think to return to, to read or say when poetry is wanted.

Surprise magnetises attention. An infant hearing an unexpected sound will stop and stare hard. The experience of surprise is itself surprising. It is also, literally, arresting: in a person strongly startled, the heart rate momentarily plummets. It's as if the whole being pauses, to better grasp what's there. Surprise does not weigh its object as "good" or "bad". Though that may follow, its essence is question, is simply 'What is it?', asked equally of any sudden change. Its facial expression, according to one researcher, is close to rapture, the openness of a baby's first awakedness, empty of self. Darwin, in his book investigating the emotions, grouped surprise with astonishment, amazement, and wonder.

In poetry, surprise deepens, gathers, and purifies attention in the same way: the mind of preconception is stopped, to allow a more acute taking-in. A taxonomy of poetic surprise covers many levels – unexpectedness can occur in word, syntax, concept, image, or rhetoric. Disruption of pattern (overt or subtle) can take place in structure, rhythm, approach, meter, or rhyme. The unlikely thing may be the choice of what is looked at. Surprise can rest entirely in a poem's textural surface or in subtext alone. One subtle path to surprise is through the movement and re-focussing of attention. Some haiku (for instance Issa's 'Don't worry, spider, I keep house casually.') simply bring the un-noticed to notice. It is as if the walls of the room you are in were suddenly to drop away and the house nextdoor – which, after all, you did know was there – were suddenly sitting com-panionably within view.

By means large or small, thought's startlements displace the self. Even the fine-grained surprise of a line's enjambment can be felt as perceptible pause and question, then an ensuing revision of mind; as occurs also in a pun, or Japanese poetry's pivot-words, both phases of mind are intended. Keats pointed to these almost intangible forms of surprise when he wrote that poetry 'surprises by fine excess'. In the density of poetry's rendering of attention, the world – and so the experiencing self – takes on a reliable abundance. It offers the same pleasure we feel before a discovered spring: we know thirst will be answered unmeagerly, with a generosity far beyond its own measure.

Surprise carries an inverse relationship to the harness of ego and will: it is the emotion of a transition not self-created. Though infants can visibly surprise themselves by sneezing, there is no self-tickling. We tend not to laugh at our own jokes, at least when alone. Yet one of the reasons creative effort is undertaken is precisely to surprise oneself by what might be found. The already-known may bring comfort, but the as-yet-undiscovered brings an enlargement of life. We are beings often skeptical of, made worried by, surprise. We are also beings who seek it out – Polynesian trans-oceanic explorers in hollowed-out logs, Atlantic City gamblers, and the mountain climber sleeping cliff-suspended on a half dozen pitons share the willingness to submit themselves to the unknown. As described earlier in this book, risk of failure – not unfamiliar to even the desk-bound – amplifies the exhilaration of success.

Surprise is the gate through which the new must pass. If something in a poem startles others, it will have startled its maker first. Robert Lowell wrote, speaking in one poem about his others, 'My Dolphin, you only guide me by surprise.' 'No surprise for the writer, no surprise for the reader,' stated Robert Frost. Poems appear to come from the self only if you do not write them. The writer knows they are gift, won from the collaboration of individual with language, self with unconscious, personal association and concept with the world's own uncontrollable materials and events. Picasso said, 'I do not seek, I find.' Insight's arrival as if from outside the self has been described not only by artists but by biologists, economists, mathematicians. The early-twentieth-century mathematical prodigy Ramanujan reported that his theorems came to him from a whispering goddess. If you leave out the goddess, the description turns out to be not uncommon among mathematicians – many radically new propositions, it seems, are proved after rather than en route to their first appearance, whole, in the mind.

At the start of considering these questions, I raised the question of abiding surprise with a friend, while walking. We reached a ridge, and I said, 'We've been here many times before, why is it always so new?' I myself was thinking of E.O Wilson's theory of sight-lines and African savannah; of the complex textures of sky, leaves, and grasses; of the role of cloud and mist in Chinese paintings. She answered, 'Because it isn't me.'

The world's beauty continually surprises, in no small part because it is not controlled by self or what self knows. Even a sand grain or pebble, considered closely, can liberate us from conscious mind's constriction, from our close-held embrace of ego's dominance over things – the proof is in poems on the subject by Zbigniew Herbert, Wisława Szymborska, Charles Simic, Carlos Drummond de Andrade. A city would serve as well; for Whitman, a country. Release of narrow view lies behind surprise in humor, intellectual riddle, tragic catharsis – why should it not lie as well behind the surprisingly perennial beauty of the objective world, which is not of our making and does not exist for our use? Astonishment's other side is powerlessness over the view.

*

Lyric epiphany is democratic, equally intimate with Aeschylus and the stand-up comic. If its effects on us seem to link it more to the former, its economy and means of meaning-making are nearer the latter. E.E. Cummings, when asked his technique in poetry, responded: 'I can express it in fifteen words, by quoting the eternal question and immortal answer of burlesque: 'Would you hit a woman with a baby? No, I'd hit her with a brick.' Like the burlesque comedian,' he went on, 'I am abnormally fond of that precision which creates movement.' The joke's technique recalls a second immortal comment, this one Groucho Marx's: 'Outside a dog, a book is a man's best friend; inside a dog, it's too dark to read.' The mechanism of the gesture is identical – a sleight-of-hand worked on a single word's disparate meanings.[1] But the example quoted by Cummings rests on slapstick's unjustified aggressions, Groucho's on its reminder of isolation and friendlessness, of the depth of a night in which a book and a dog are the only two options and even they are then stripped away. His invention holds word-wit in its right hand; in its left, the sufferings of Jonah and Job.

Familiar jokes can continue to evoke laughter for the same reasons known poems continue to move and surprise. We perennially fall for what enlists us into an experience so simply and seductively presented that we cannot not enter through the offered, open door. Neither a poem's nor a joke's reason for being can be found except by remaking the motions of mind that create it. A joke's punch-line, like a poem's meaning, is not in its words, but in what we make of those words. As with poems, our amnesia to certain jokes is almost complete; when it

51

isn't, we sometimes laugh harder, at the inertia of prat-fallible mind. The performing arts – which include comedy, poetry, music, dance, and magic, as well as theater – ask of us not only the theater's well known suspension of disbelief, but also suspension of foreknowledge. All partake of ritual: the reenactment of and entrance into a mystery that can be touched but not possessed.

'Wit' was once a synonym for simple 'knowing'. Groucho's words feel close to those of a poem not only in their undertow sadness, but in that undertow's very existence, in its challenge to deep preconception. Jokes are supposed to be funny, are they not? Yet what makes a truly good joke good is precisely that it is not merely mechanically funny; it also shows us something both discomforting and true. We are alone. Inside a dog, and us, it is dark.

The more surprise in good poetry is looked at, the more its work seems close to the work of the comic and trickster: it argues against those things we most think we know. It is when unexamined assumptions of mind and nature are shaken that we are most moved, in the arts as in science. Against gravity and entropic loss, a poem proposes the levitations of fine excess and gratuitous beauty – sound-trance's memorability; the aerial devices of implication; metaphor's democratic conjugation with all existence; the praise of whatever is for what it is. In a painting, a small square of sunlight rests on the rounded shoulder of a glass vase, preserved impossibly against time's passage; the pause in a piece of music by Mozart stops the heart for no reason except that it is there. Against transience, art provides a witnessing endurance; against the stringencies of survival, it offers the moment's dalliance or chosen disappearance. The love poem born of unfulfilled desire embraces its own longing. The love poem of fulfillment carries somewhere within it, however lightly, the shadow of time and death. A painted apple cannot be eaten. As evolution's creatures, we align with goal-attainment, self-protection, and the useful. The part of art which is art, and not device, unshackles us from usefulness almost entirely.

*

If we are to test these ideas upon poems, the recalcitrant case interests most, and so in place of more obvious examples, I have chosen three works whose challenges to preconception both differ from one another and are not easy to name. C.P. Cavafy's 'Ithaka' is as good a place as any to start – a poem that retains through many readings the power to peel the soul freshly from sleep.

Ithaka

As you set out for Ithaka
hope your road is a long one,
full of adventure, full of discovery.
Laistrygonians, Cyclops,
angry Poseidon – don't be afraid of them:
you'll never find things like that on your way
as long as you keep your thoughts raised high,
as long as a rare excitement
stirs your spirit and your body.
Laistrygonians, Cyclops,
wild Poseidon – you won't encounter them
unless you bring them along inside your soul,
unless your soul sets them up in front of you.

Hope your road is a long one.
May there be many summer mornings when,
with what pleasure, what joy,
you enter harbors you're seeing for the first time;
may you stop at Phoenician trading stations
to buy fine things,
mother of pearl and coral, amber and ebony.
sensual perfume of every kind –
as many sensual perfumes as you can;
and may you visit many Egyptian cities
to learn and go on learning from their scholars.

Keep Ithaka always in your mind.
Arriving there is what you're destined for.
But don't hurry the journey at all.
Better if it lasts for years,
so you're old by the time you reach the island,
wealthy with all you've gained on the way,
not expecting Ithaka to make you rich.

Ithaka gave you the marvelous journey.
Without her you wouldn't have set out.
She has nothing left to give you now.

And if you find her poor, Ithaka won't have fooled you.
Wise as you will have become, so full of experience,
you'll have understood by then what these Ithakas mean.[2]

(tr. by Edmund Keeley and Philip Sherrard)

Cavafy's stamp of mind is hermetic, not martial. Encountering 'Ithaka' even in translation, the self knows itself readjusted; yet it is difficult to articulate quite where the transformation lies. Modest of surface, perambulative, the poem's language is plain, its tone unheated even when speaking of marvel; and though sufficient detail is given for the narrative, sensuous, and image-making mind to be fed, even these offerings are evocative but not detailed. Summer mornings, exotic places, mother of pearl, ebony, and perfume – these are semaphores for the sensory world, glittering samples flashed on a street corner to pull in a mark. On first look, too, the poem seems filled more with abstraction and the hypnosis of repetition than with identifiable revelation. 'Full of adventure, full of discovery'; 'with what pleasure, what joy' – such paralleled doublings with small variation are among Cavafy's most customary gestures. The poem refers to monsters and adventure, but its terrors are so mildly murmured, they pass unfelt.

But look again: 'As you set out for Ithaka, hope your road is a long one.' Odysseus's journey was indeed long, but its ten-year duration was not (despite the interval with Circe) Odysseus's stated desire. To make it so is Cavafy's invention. Slipped in so simply and quietly that one hardly notices what it says, or that it is the only phrase in the poem repeated exactly, 'Ithaka''s most overt statement cuts sharply against the grain. Hope of delay and long travel not only inverts cultural attitudes toward pursuit and goal, it unravels the fundamental dynamics of our Metazoan animal nature. Desire, ingenuity, and effort aim in mammalian life toward resolution, not their own prolonging.

Even the poem's relationship to its title embodies its central point: the city – in this poem – is never reached. Cavafy is like the magician whose gestures are made so far out in the open they are almost impossible to see: each time, we feel their outcome as surprise. By this smoke-and-mirror invisibility, the central imperative skirts both the didactic and staling. Still, if I am right that a poem's volatility stems from the inability to hold its full meaning in mind, the overt statement cannot be the sole source of 'Ithaka''s power. Nor is 'Hope your road is a long one' the triggering phrase by which the poem is recalled. While there are other counter-wisdoms (most sharply the suggestion that all monsters are self-created), the plumb weight of full revelation falls at the end. For me, the words by which this poem returns to mind are 'Ithaka gave you the marvelous journey', and what follows: 'And if you find her poor, Ithaka won't have fooled you. / Wise as you will have become, so full of experience, / you'll have understood by then what these Ithakas mean.' The lines are a small brutality, chilling in their knocking aside of what once was desired. The feminine pronoun does its work as well. In it is the one reminder that it is Penelope also being dismissed, and with her all our felt, human connections to family and home.

A ritual must be passed through, not glimpsed through a door. However efficient a single syllable may sometimes be, 'Ithaka's' entirety is needed to make its journey; this could not be a poem of five or seven lines. Ordinarily we think repetition must be antithetical to surprise or intensification – how can the already known bring fresh news? Yet when a clown attempts and fails repeatedly, each time more puzzled, the audience laughs more loudly each time. Repetition allows saturation, and is not in any case the same as a thing said once. (Think of Charlie Brown's faith that Lucy will someday hold the football in place for his kick, a motif made only more meaningful because the betrayal has happened so many times before.) By 'Ithaka''s conclusion, the effects of recurrence and allusion have deepened the poem's revelation as long rubbing with sheep's wool and beeswax deepens the grain and color of a table while giving it shine. The experience of recognition, of seeing fully what was always there to be seen – in life, as in the poem – is as much as anything 'Ithaka''s, and poetry's, surprise.

A different purchase on surprise can be found in Seamus Heaney's 'Oysters', a poem that exemplifies the close-woven attention to experience and language which, fully followed, leads to a complex liberation for the writer, for the reader:

Oysters

Our shells clacked on the plates.
My tongue was a filling estuary,
My palate hung with starlight:
As I tasted the salty Pleiades
Orion dipped his foot into the water.

Alive and violated,
They lay on their beds of ice:
Bivalves: the split bulb
and philandering sigh of ocean.
Millions of them ripped and shucked and scattered.

We had driven to that coast
Through flowers and limestone
And there we were, toasting friendship,
Laying down a perfect memory
In the cool of thatch and crockery.

Over the Alps, packed deep in hay and snow,
The Romans hauled their oysters south to Rome:
I saw damp panniers disgorge
The frond-lipped, brine-stung
Glut of privilege

And was angry that my trust could not repose
In the clear light, like poetry or freedom
Leaning in from the sea. I ate the day
Deliberately, that its tang
Might quicken me all into verb, pure verb.[3]

We stand in this poem with a master of shaking things together – the personal with the historical, the local with the large, the life of the body that eats with the life of the feeling heart and thoughtful mind. Selective intelligence manifests as well – part of this poem's specific gravity is its confident leaving out of the inessential. The resultant speed is discernable even in the first line: 'Our shells clacked on the plates.' We notice first the sure onomotopoeia of 'clacked' against 'plates'. Less obvious is the way the sentence plunges the reader into its scene *in medias res*: the oysters have been already swallowed. The shells are 'ours', and empty.

I articulate the detail to make something clear. A poem's comprehension does not require conscious consent. We extrapolate the existence of the riddle, not just its solution, from the clues, in a process mostly beneath the surface of awareness. That this happens in itself surprises: what was the knowledge doing, and where was it doing it, before we knew it was there? Poetry shares the rhetorical strategies Freud pointed to in dreams: compression, displacement, metaphoric image, pun, and wit. Each relies on the mind knowing more than it knows, more than is outwardly given. And in the case of poetry, relies on the transmission of this surplus of knowledge from one mind into another so tactfully it need not ever break the surface to have its effect.

In its second line, 'Oysters' turns to metaphor, a device centered on an unexpected juxtaposition whose implications are instantaneously and subliminally understood. Good metaphor renews, opens, and extends perception. The surprise of 'My tongue was a filling estuary' lies in its joining of human body and body of water, distant in size and conceptual category both; its aptness comes from the recognition of likeness between tongue flooded with oyster brine and riverine inlet filling with ocean.

To read a poem is both to savor its particularities and to make of them a wholeness. Reaching the next surprising statement, 'My palate hung with starlight', the reader immediately casts the filling estuary into darkness and recognises both starlight and salt (which will not be explicitly named until the following line) as sharing whiteness. But we also feel the poem increase in space and time, its images moving from shells and plate, tongue and palate, into the planet-scale largenesses of sea, earth, and sky, then myth. Experientially, though, the movement is in part contrapuntal – the intimate interior expands to hold estuary and stars. Not only tongue but the self's capacities are altered.

The second stanza exchanges pleasure for the violence eating also is: a rapacity multiplied beyond counting. 'Alive and violated' is simple fact in oysters eaten raw, but the grammar governs not only the oysters: it is the Pleiades, the seven sisters pursued by Orion, who lie now as bivalves, opened on beds of ice. In a world whose beings live and die, the savoring of abundance is not far from acknowledgement of grief. The stanza's music holds the change as well. Long *i*-sounds give way to a short-vowelled, single line abruptness: 'Millions of them ripped and shucked and scattered.' Parataxis here is speech condensed by pain. The description surely foreshadows the anger later on in the poem.

Next come flowers and limestone, friendship, memory, toasting – a day again close to Edenic. The crockery is unbroken, the thatch unburned. The fourth stanza, though, makes a turn of the kind made formal in sonnets: an addition that both quickens thought and brings a question needing answer. Imperial violence is a subject not broachable by a Northern Irish poet in the 1970s without calling to mind the more proximate history as well. The speaker's welcome coolness under roof thatch now echoes that of the oysters hauled south, under their snow and hay.

Explicit upsurge of anger brings to consciousness the poem's full dialectical range – the consuming of oysters is an act of human and ecological pillage; the communion of friendship in one place cannot erase suffering in another; if there are Pleiades, there is a pursuing Orion who drives them. And yet consenting to the world we are given is what we do. And more than consent. The day's tang is answered with what Heaney described, in a letter speaking of this poem, as 'a certain ferocity or bite called for in [a poet's] vocation'. The promise of the poem's final word leads both toward the action of 'verb' and toward what is verbal: a poetry alert to the work of witness, a poet unable to blind himself or be silent before what he sees.

Here we can see that a good poem's fracture of familiarity and assumption need not be a single, large countervalence. 'Oysters''s unexpectedness rests not so much in a single extractable concept (though the conceptual and an evaluating moral presence are each fiercely there) but in multiple movements of mind which, line by line, are agile leaps in directions impossible to predict, toward a whole not subject to easy summation. Its volatility lies in a balance precise and exacting, momentarily found amid imbalances fundamental, insoluble and continuing.

The last poem I would like to look at for its surprises is Robert Frost's brief, adamantine 'Nothing Gold Can Stay'.

Nothing Gold Can Stay

Nature's first green is gold,
Her hardest hue to hold.

Her early leaf's a flower;
But only so an hour.
Then leaf subsides to leaf.
So Eden sank to grief,
So dawn goes down to day.
Nothing gold can stay.[4]

Frost's poem is not unlike Cavafy's – a round-form poem in which the end and beginning appear identical, yet whose reader, going from point A to point A, knows herself or himself completely changed. As with 'Ithaka', the basic counter-statement is set down at the start so clearly and quietly the mind has trouble noticing that it *is* counter: we take the title at face value, without protest. Yet isn't gold the very archetype of that which does in fact stay, untarnished, bright against time? The poem's formal structure similarly belies its radical dismantling: four end-stopped and straight-rhymed couplets, mostly iambic trimeter, though the first and last lines each begin with an emphasising trochee. It is a music of orderly, reassuring recurrence, a poem any child could be put to bed by. So, of course, is 'Rock a bye, baby' – a lullaby of genuinely Frostian temperament, with its gleeful conclusion: 'Down will come baby, cradle and all.'

'Nothing Gold Can Stay' wears the structure of logical syllogism. A poem of premise and conclusion, of data and proof, its first half establishes its *bona fides*, so to speak. Inarguable that new leaves, undeepened by chlorophyll and sun, are not yet green; that the first whorls of an apple tree's foliage are shaped like an opening bud; that these things will soon change. Yet even these opening lines offer the small-scale shock we now recognise as a certain kind of recognition: a making conscious of what was already there to be seen. Frost then begins to quietly alter the contract. Or not so quietly – 'Then leaf subsides to leaf' is a dazzling undoing. Its thought is the first to be held to a single line, and the following rhyme-word, 'grief', is prefigured by the pattern-breaking pause: its diminishment so strongly felt, no comment can follow. The parataxis, like that in 'Oysters', is pain-drawn. A statement that by ordinary logic should be without meaning instead holds perception of loss so large that only spareness can convey it. Yet by any usual assumptions and measure, 'subsides' is wrong: the leaf is growing. It is by Frost's measuring as poet, not farmer, that increase is loss.

Each of the following verbs echoes the downward direction of 'subsides'. That Eden might sink to grief is plausible – the story is after all referred to as The Fall – but that dawn *goes down* to day is once again entirely counter to usual description. The conscious mind doesn't register this as reversal; the heart does. 'Inception is loss.' The thought is slipped in as only a very sharp knife can be, and one feels the effect only after. E.E. Cummings's formulation describes well what this is: a precision creating movement. The poem's change of grammar is also precise, and bifurcating. '*So* Eden sank to grief' moves from leaf-description to suffering in the grammar of logical conclusion (if 'so' is read as 'therefore') but also in the grammar of example and illustration (if it is read as 'likewise'). In the first, the loss of paradise is the poem's focus, in the second, it is no more important than a leaf's change of form. The gesture repeats in the following line. And there is the music, too, to be noticed: the repeated, long *e*-sounds of Eden and grief succumb to softly recurring *d*s against the shift of vowels in 'dawn' and 'down' and then the long-vowelled 'day'.

'*Nothing gold can stay.*' The statement's proof lies first with a leaf's small loss of shape and color, then with the fallen world; finally even the day's ordinary increase of physical light is described as a failure, the radiant possible becoming only what happens. By the time the title line returns, the quantity of loss it holds is beyond reckoning. It is not just the outer; it is we ourselves who are dismantled of both our first brightness and the hope of lasting. We, not gold, are what goes. The devastation is beautiful and complete.

Beauty is what Frost, and poetry, leaves us. The surprising beauty of truth fully acknowledged, well told and also well tolled – as in what a bell does, as in a tally honestly kept.

While poetry reminds of the uselessness of the useful, it reminds as well of the usefulness of the useless. It reminds, that is, that existence itself is sufficient. The reasoning of great poetry transcends reason because reason – a faculty rooted in the attainment of goal and its own perpetuation – cannot and does not encompass the whole of life. Through a good poem's eyes we see the world liberated from what we would have it do. Existence does not guarantee us destination, nor trust, nor equity, nor one moment beyond this instant's almost weightless duration. It is a triteness to say that the only thing to be counted upon is that what you count on will not be what comes. Utilitarian truths evaporate: we die. Poems allow us not only to bear the tally and toll of our transience, but to perceive, within their continually surprising abundance, a path through the grief of that insult into joy.

I began these considerations believing the transcending knowledge of poems is a singularly human liberation; that poetic epiphany, by loosening the psyche from the grip of expectation and purposeful pursuit, is a capacity of knowing entirely unique to our own kind. I still think this is so: if there is a poetry of dolphins, ravens, and elephants, it is not like ours. But something else seems possible as well – that the opposite is also true, that the peculiarly human phenomenon is the grip held on the heart by goal-seeking, end-weddedness, purpose, and that what good poems restore us to is something close to what is meant by 'animal joy'. They allow us to see the leaf's passage from gold to green and mourn neither, to taste an oyster for both the history of rapacity and its salt. Poetry's surprisingly purposeless purpose, now as in Homeric Greece, is to restore to us the amplitude and exuberance of the Ithakan journey, even when knowing that inside a dog it is dark.

NOTES

1. Interestingly, both cases rely on prepositions: in the first case, 'with', in the second, 'outside'. English prepositions reify what is more fluid in languages using inflection, and reification always opens the gate to the comic.

2. *Collected Poems by* C.P. Cavafy, revised edition, edited by George Savidis, translated by Edmund Keeley and Philip Sherrard (Princeton: Princeton University Press, 1992).

3. *Opened Ground: Poems 1966-1996* (London: Faber and Faber, 1998).

4. *Selected Poems* by Robert Frost (New York: Holt, Rinehart and Winston, 1963).

Jane Hirshfield was born in 1953 in New York City and received her A.B. from Princeton University in 1973. She has lived in northern California since 1974. In 2005 Bloodaxe Books published *Each Happiness Ringed by Lions: Selected Poems*, her first British publication, drawing on five award-winning American collections: *Alaya* (1982), *Of Gravity & Angels* (1988), *The October Palace* (1994), *The Lives of the Heart* (1997) and *Given Sugar, Given Salt* (2001). This was followed by four later collections from Bloodaxe in the UK: *After* (2006), a Poetry Book Society Choice shortlisted for the T.S. Eliot Prize; *Come, Thief* (2012); *The Beauty* (2015); and *Ledger* (2020). In 2008 Bloodaxe and Newcastle University published Jane Hirshfield's Newcastle/Bloodaxe Poetry Lectures, *Hiddenness, Surprise, Uncertainty: Three Generative Energies of Poetry*.

She has also published two collections of essays, *Nine Gates: Entering the Mind of Poetry*, (HarperCollins, 1997) and *Ten Windows: How Great Poems Transform the World* (Knopf, 2015), and has edited and served as co-translator for several acclaimed and much reprinted volumes collecting the work of women poets of the past: *The Ink Dark Moon: Love Poems by Ono no Komachi and Izumi Shikibu, Women of the Ancient Court of Japan* (Scribner's, 1988; Vintage Classics, 1990); *Women in Praise of the Sacred: 43 Centuries of Spiritual Poetry by Women* (HarperCollins, 1994); and *Mirabai: Ecstatic Poems* (Beacon Press, 2004). Her own poetry has been translated into Polish by Czesław Miłosz (among others), who also wrote the introduction for her bestselling Polish Selected Poems, published by Znak in 2002.

She has taught at the University of California, Berkeley, at Stanford University and elsewhere, and has held many residencies. She has had fellowships from the Guggenheim and Rockefeller foundations, the National Endowment for the Arts, and the Academy of American Poets. In 2012 she was elected a Chancellor of the Academy of American Poets, and in 2019 she was inducted into the American Academy of Arts and Sciences.

www.ingramcontent.com/pod-product-compliance
Lightning Source LLC
Jackson TN
JSHW080855211224
75817JS00002B/61